SPOTLIGHT ON CHILDREN'S AUTHORS

JACQUELINE WOODSON

LAURA L. SULLIVAN

Cavendish Square
New York

Published in 2015 by Cavendish Square Publishing, LLC
243 5th Avenue, Suite 136, New York, NY 10016

Website: cavendishsq.com

This publication represents the opinions and views of the author based on his or her personal experience, knowledge, and research. The information in this book serves as a general guide only. The author and publisher have used their best efforts in preparing this book and disclaim liability rising directly or indirectly from the use and application of this book.

CPSIA Compliance Information: Batch #WS14CSQ

All websites were available and accurate when this book was sent to press.

Library of Congress Cataloging-in-Publication Data

Sullivan, Laura Lee.
Jacqueline Woodson / by Laura Lee Sullivan.
p. cm. — (Spotlight on children's authors)
Includes index.
ISBN 978-1-62712-855-1 (hardcover) ISBN 978-1-62712-857-5 (paperback) ISBN 978-1-62712-856-8 (ebook)
1.Woodson, Jacqueline — Juvenile literature. 2. Authors, American — 20th century — Biography — Juvenile literature. 3. African American women authors — Biography — Juvenile literature. I. Sullivan, Laura L. (Laura Lee) II. Title.

PS3573.O64524 Z68 2015
813—d23

Editorial Director: Dean Miller
Editor: Andrew Coddington
Senior Copy Editor: Wendy A. Reynolds
Art Director: Jeffrey Talbot

Designer: Amy Greenan
Production Manager: Jennifer Ryder-Talbot
Production Editor: David McNamara
Photo Research: J8 Media

Printed in the United States of America

CONTENTS

INTRODUCTION:

Sweet Beginnings

In 1965, an adorable two-year-old girl was selected to be the face of Alaga Syrup. A series of advertisements featuring her charming, impish grin ran in the popular monthly magazine *Ebony*. Though she was only a toddler, she seemed so mature that many of the ads portrayed her as a schoolgirl. "I wish they had

"I wish...

they had Alaga syrup at school too"

Alaga Syrup is rich in wholesome, energy-giving dextrose . . . that is so good for the children like Jaqueline Woodson pictured above. The sweet natural juices of field-ripened sugar cane give Alaga that smooth sweet taste on waffles, pancakes and biscuits. Write for our free recipe folder "Breakfast in a Jiffy." You will love the new ideas for getting Alaga flavor in a variety of breakfast dishes.

ALAGA SYRUP COMPANY, P.O. Box 791, Montgomery, Alabama 36102

Alaga Syrup at school, too!" the caption said, even though the little girl wouldn't start school for another three years.

The ad didn't just feature her face—it included her name, too. It sang the praises of sugar with copy like, "Alaga Syrup is rich in wholesome, energy-giving dextrose... that is so good for the children like Jacqueline Woodson pictured above." Being the face of Alaga Syrup was not only Jacqueline Woodson's first job, it was also the first time her name had appeared in print. It certainly wouldn't be her last.

Little Jacqueline would go on to become one of today's most beloved — and controversial — authors. Her name would grace the jackets of more than two dozen books for children and young adults. She would win many accolades, including the prestigious Coretta Scott King Award. Her books would inspire— and they would be banned. Jacqueline Woodson breaks barriers in the publishing world because of what she writes about, as well as because of who she is.

Jacqueline spent some of her childhood in Brooklyn, and now makes it her home. It is a place well-known for artists and writers. In fact, it is jokingly said that when you cross the Brooklyn Bridge (pictured) they hand you an MFA (Master's of Fine Arts degree).

Chapter 1
THE GIRL WHO TOLD LIES

Jacqueline Woodson was born February 12, 1963, in Columbus, Ohio. Later, her family moved, and Jacqueline lived part of the year in South Carolina, and part in Brooklyn, New York. The two places seemed like entirely different worlds to young Jacqueline, and she loved them both. "The south was so lush and so slow moving and so much about community," she said. By contrast, "the city was thriving and fast-moving and electric." Brooklyn was also much more diverse, exposing Jacqueline to many different cultures. "On the block where I grew up, there were German people, people from the Dominican Republic, people from Puerto Rico, African Americans from the south, Caribbean-Americans, Asians." Brooklyn proved to be an eclectic melting pot of influences for the budding young writer.

Whether it was a result of her surroundings or not, Jacqueline did fall in love with writing at a very young age. She might not have known how to shape words into a story, or have had any premonition about her future career, but she recognized the amazing power of words at the age of three. The epiphany came when her older sister taught her how to write her name. She wasn't content to write only her first name, though; she had to write the whole thing, the representation of her full identity. Her three-year-old fingers carefully wrote every letter: Jacqueline Amanda Woodson.

Describing how she felt when she wrote her name, Jacqueline says: "I just loved the power of being able to put a letter on the page and that letter meaning something. It was the physical act of writing for me that happened first. Not so much telling stories, but actually having the tools with which to create a landscape of words."

From that moment, it seems, she never stopped writing. "I wrote on everything and everywhere," she said. "I wrote on paper bags and my shoes and denim binders." All that writing even got her into trouble as a kid, including writing her name, which had almost magical significance to her. One day, her uncle caught her scrawling her name in graffiti on the wall of a building. "It was not pretty for me when my mother found out," Jacqueline said.

From writing her name, Jacqueline soon turned to writing stories—everywhere. She would use chalk to scribble stories on sidewalks for the whole neighborhood to see. In school, she would write miniscule tales in the margins of her notebooks. It gave her a thrill to watch each story grow: "I loved and still love watching words flower into sentences and sentences blossom into stories."

Young Jacqueline didn't just write stories; she told them, too. However, she admits, they weren't so much stories as lies. She didn't necessarily tell whoppers out of malice, but from the sheer joy of creating something and seeing how realistic and believable

Jacqueline's first acknowledgment for writing was for a poem about Martin Luther King, Jr. It was so good that some people thought she didn't really write it.

she could make it. It was a skill that would serve her well in her writing career. "I loved lying and getting away with it," she said. She would tell taller and taller tales, and watch her friends' eyes grow wide with amazement. Sometimes she couldn't fool them, but most of the time she could. "Of course I got in trouble for lying, but I didn't stop until fifth grade," Jacqueline said. That was when she learned to call lies by another name, and put them to better use.

Jacqueline's first writing experience was a bittersweet one that could have turned her off writing forever if it had ended a little differently. She wrote a poem about Martin Luther King, Jr. that showed so much talent that her teachers didn't believe she actually wrote it. She was accused of plagiarism, and it was only after "lots of brouhaha," or excitement, that people finally accepted a little girl could have so much skill at writing.

SOME OF JACQUELINE'S
FAVORITE THINGS

Writers rarely have one-word answers to anything. On her website, Jacqueline goes into detail about a few of her favorite things. For example, her favorite color "used to be blue, but now it's most of the time green. I like earth tones more than pastels, and I love stripes!"

Jacqueline's favorite food does get a one-word answer: pizza. She said she could eat pizza seven days a week and never get sick of it. Her least-favorite foods make up a much longer list, which includes "avocado, mushrooms, artichokes, raspberries, papaya, meat, Brussels sprouts, alfalfa sprouts, oatmeal, mussels, sea bass..." She adds that the list is actually much longer.

You might guess that Jacqueline's favorite subject in school was English—and you'd be right! She also loved gym, Spanish, and "anything that allowed us to dance or jump around." Math and science were the subjects she liked least.

She also has several favorite places to write, including, "anywhere on the Cape [Cape Cod, Massachusetts] where there are dunes nearby," and in her hometown of Brooklyn. She does a lot of her writing on a special yellow chair in her office. When she writes by hand, the paper has to be turned sideways. When she was a kid, she wrote with the paper all the way upside-down.

When asked if she has a favorite character in her books, she said, "I like them all for different reasons. It's like having a bunch of kids... each one is special for their own reasons, and I don't think I could choose among them."

That poem won Jacqueline her first real acknowledgment as a writer. She received a very appropriate prize for a young wordsmith—a game of Scrabble—as well as a great deal of local acclaim. Not too long after that, she tried her hand at writing again, this time with a short story. She found it had the power to transform.

Jacqueline's fifth grade teacher was known for being so grumpy that she hardly ever smiled. However, when she read Jacqueline's story, her lips actually curled into a grin and she uttered rare words of praise, saying, "This is really good." It made Jacqueline start to believe in herself, too. Before it happened, she describes herself as having been a "skinny little girl in the back of the classroom who was always getting into trouble for talking or missed homework assignments." After receiving that compliment from her hard-to-please teacher, however, she found that she "sat up a little straighter, folded [her] hands on the desk, smiled, and began to believe in [herself]."

Her fifth grade teacher's words also changed Jacqueline's view of her frequent lies. "I was well on my way to understanding that a lie on the page was a whole different animal," she said. It meant a new outlook for Jacqueline. Her lies suddenly had merit, and people began to understand why a girl with so much imagination simply had to come up with stories. They let her do what she loved. As Jacqueline said, "a lie on the page meant lots of independent time to create your stories and the freedom to sit hunched over the pages of your notebook without people thinking you were strange."

As a teen, Jacqueline discovered African
American novelists, such as Toni Morrison,
who would become lifelong favorites.

Chapter 2
A DREAM DEFERRED?

Some authors fall in love with reading first, and only later realize that they might have the ability to create stories themselves. Jacqueline discovered the power of writing first, but was a little slower to fully embrace reading. It wasn't that she didn't adore books, it was only that the adults in her life were so adamant about her reading that her naturally rebellious streak had to surface every once in a while.

"My mom didn't allow us to watch much television," Jacqueline said. Instead, her mother was always telling the children, "You need to be reading!" That phrase, Jacqueline said, made her very cranky as a kid.

All the same, books were a huge part of her childhood. Jacqueline was raised by her single mother and grandmother. Her parents had split up when Jacqueline was only two months old. Her mother worked, and after school, Jacqueline, her older brother and sister, and her younger brother, always did the same thing: They went to the Washington Irving branch of the Brooklyn Public Library. It was their own after-school program, a place of safety and knowledge.

Every day they walked from school to the local library, which was about a block away from their house on Madison Street. "There we did our homework, and when done, we read." Their mom would pick them up at 5:45, just before the library closed at 6:00. Her mother encouraged all of her children to become lifelong readers. "She made sure we all had library cards," Jacqueline said, "and that they were in good standing," free from any fines for overdue books. Jacqueline explained, "We had many books at home (mostly ones we borrowed from the library)."

Jacqueline spent most of her time in the picture book section, reading the same books over and over again. She said she was a very slow reader as a small child, and stuck to her favorites, the books that never got boring no matter how many times she read them. Even later in life, she stuck to her habit of constantly re-reading some of her favorite books. It helped her become a great writer—by doing this, her favorite authors became her teachers. "Every time you revisit a book you get something else out of it," Jacqueline said. "The more familiar I got with them, the more accessible the act of writing was."

As she read more and more, though, Jacqueline noticed a disturbing trend. It was very hard to find books about people who looked like her. Jacqueline is African American, and the majority of the characters in the books she found in the library and in school were white. Finding books that represented her experience was a challenge. "You had to search for the literature for people of color by people of color," she said.

One of the books she really couldn't stand was also one of the few to feature African American characters—*Sounder*. It was written by a white man. "It was supposed to be my people and it wasn't, and I couldn't tell how it wasn't," she said of the book, which is about a family of sharecroppers in the South in the first half of the twentieth century. "So I felt... like something was wrong with me. As an adult," she said, "I realized that no one had a name except the dog." The novel was bleak, and the characters not only desperately poor, but sad. "They were supposed to be southerners," Jacqueline said, "but they never touched each other, and you know southerners are always hugging and kissing and saying, 'look how you've grown!'"

When Jacqueline got a little older, she discovered authors of color who were to become both her perennial favorites and her inspiration, including Toni Morrison (*Beloved*, *The Bluest Eye*), Virginia Hamilton (*Zeely*, *M.C. Higgins, the Great*), and James Baldwin (*Go Tell It on the Mountain*). As Jacqueline said, "I think Baldwin was such a big influence on me because he was writing about people in the city. I think he came closest to who I was, growing up."

Jacqueline always wrote as a child. "I wrote poetry and songs and silly rhymes all the time because I loved doing so," she said. "I made up lots of stories to entertain my siblings with, and I was always excited about any kind of writing assignment our teachers gave us." Still, Jacqueline thought that, at the most, writing would turn out to be a hobby—something she did in her spare time. It was a matter of practicality, not dreams and desires.

JACQUELINE'S FAVORITE CHILDHOOD BOOKS

Jacqueline is often asked about her favorite books as a child. Though her answers vary somewhat in different interviews, these are some of the books she mentions most often. They taught her about herself, and also opened up the world to her.

Stevie, by John Steptoe, is a picture book about a little boy who first resents a neighbor who comes to stay with his family, then misses him when he leaves. She liked it because, "they talked like I did, they were brown like I was brown," which was hard for her to find in a book when she was growing up.

Jacqueline also related to *Are You There God? It's Me, Margaret* by Judy Blume for many reasons, including because she was "flat chested like Margaret."

Jacqueline spent much of her childhood in the south, and *Roll of Thunder, Hear My Cry*, with its southern setting, spoke to her. The Newbery Medal-winning book by Mildred D. Taylor is about a close-knit African American family in an era of brutal racism.

In Virginia Hamilton's *Zeely*, a young African American girl who loves to create fantasies visits her uncle's farm for the summer, where she meets a regal woman named Zeely. "*Zeely* was one of the first books I read that was by an African American about African American people," Jacqueline said.

Despite her love of both reading and writing, her career path wasn't ever a straight line. Her mother and grandmother discouraged her from pursuing writing as a full-time career, even while they seemed to guide her down that path by encouraging her to read and supporting her writing as a child. They might have wanted her to read and write, but they also knew how financially uncertain a writing career can be, and hoped she'd pick something more stable and reliable for a primary job.

"Of course, my big dream was to only write," she said. In an ideal world, she thought, that's what she could do for her one and only career. However, the world is rarely ideal, and it took her a while to get there. "Even as my mom and grandma discouraged me from being a writer as a career, they were subversively (whether they knew this or not) showing me the road to life as a writer."

One of her high school teachers seemed more inclined to direct her toward her dreams. Her high school English teacher Mr. Miller gave her this career advice: "When you choose a career, choose something that you feel passionate about, because you're going to be doing it for the rest of your life."

That was a defining moment for Jacqueline. It was the moment she fully realized that writing was the thing she loved doing more than anything else.

Jacqueline attended Adelphi University,
where she studied English.

Chapter 3
THE DREAM COMES TRUE

Jacqueline decided to study English in college. It was a natural choice for someone who loved reading and writing and who didn't care much for math and science. (In fact, she says she hated those subjects, and found it hard to sit still in school or anywhere else unless she was reading a book.) At first, she thought she would train to be a teacher to give back some of what her favorite teachers had given her.

While in college, she was still thinking of writing as a hobby. In her junior year at Adelphi University, she started working on her first novel, *Last Summer With Maizon*. While penning that manuscript, she hit some obstacles. She found out why it is so hard to be a professional writer: "You're writing, you're coasting, and you're thinking, *This is the best thing I've ever written, and it's coming so easily, and these characters are so great.* You put it aside for whatever reason, and you open it up a week later and the characters have turned to cardboard and the book has completely fallen apart."

The hardest part of writing, she thinks, is going back over something that seemed so easy to write, so perfect in the first draft,

Jacqueline found success when an editor happened to hear a reading of her manuscript at a writing class.

then having to figure out what the problems really are and correct them. That, she thinks, is what separates the dilettantes, or people who write as a hobby, from the professional writers.

"That's the moment of truth for every writer," she said. "Can I go on from here and make this book into something?" That, she thinks, is the reason why so many people who would like to be writers have several unfinished manuscripts hidden away in drawers. The first chapters, even the first draft, are relatively easy. It's what comes afterward that takes real dedication and hard work.

When she left college, Jacqueline accepted a job with Kirchoff/ Wohlberg, a packaging company that specialized in children's books. The company was working on a project that included writing standardized tests for California school children. For part of the reading test, Jacqueline used an excerpt of her novel, *Last Summer with Maizon*.

That snippet of text caught the attention of Liza Pulitzer-Voges, a children's literary agent who was working for Kirchoff/Wohlberg at the time. She asked to see the complete manuscript, and liked it so much that she wanted to submit it to editors. However, it wasn't quite the time for Jacqueline to find fame yet. Only one editor thought the manuscript showed promise. That editor wrote a three-page letter filled with thoughts on how to improve the book. The only problem was, the editor had taken seven months to get back to Jacqueline, which she thought was far too long and didn't bode well for their future working relationship. She wanted an editor who took her writing seriously enough not to keep her on tenterhooks for months on end.

She might not have been offered a book deal, but the experience made Jacqueline take her writing more seriously. She signed up for Margaret "Bunny" Gable's writing class at the New School in New York City, and learned all she could about the craft of writing from one of the best teachers in the field. She didn't just receive instruction, but was encouraged to share her work with her teacher and other students, and benefitted from their feedback.

One lucky night, Bebe Willoughby, an editor from Delacorte, sat in on the writing class. As it happened, Bunny was reading part of *Last Summer with Maizon* aloud. The editor liked what she heard, and asked Liza Pulitzer-Voges to forward the complete manuscript to her office. She loved it so much that she bought it. Before it was published, Willoughby left Delacorte, but another editor, Wendy Lamb, picked up the book. It was published in 1991. Wendy Lamb proved such an advocate for Jacqueline's work that she remained her editor for the next six books.

Wendy Lamb was a very hands-on editor, which is exactly what Jacqueline thought she needed at the time. She was new to the game and a little uncertain about what was allowed in children's books. "I had this idea that there were certain things you couldn't say," Jacqueline explained. "And Wendy said, basically, 'Nothing you can do is wrong.'" Her words and wisdom gave Jacqueline the freedom to explore the many deep and controversial topics that her novels are known for.

From her editor, Jacqueline also learned that all-important but often overlooked part of writing: revisions and edits. At that early stage, she wanted someone to walk her through the manuscript, holding her hand as she searched for ways to polish and perfect it. With Lamb's help, Jacqueline managed to shape her manuscript exactly as she thought it was meant to be, bringing all of her messages sharply into focus. While Lamb guided her, she made a point of telling Jacqueline that one day she wouldn't need anyone to help her through that arduous final process. She'd be able to do it herself.

Last Summer with Maizon is about two eleven-year-old girls, Margaret and Maizon, who are best friends. When Margaret's father dies, and Maizon moves away to a ritzy boarding school,

Margaret has to figure out who she is without the people closest to her. After the book was published, it received critical acclaim for featuring interesting and realistic female characters with fully realized relationships.

Last Summer with Maizon was exactly the kind of book Jacqueline would have wished for when she was a young girl. "Growing up, there were very few books about black girls, and even fewer about people like the people I knew in my neighborhood in Brooklyn. I wanted to write about the people I loved and the neighborhood that had been my home for many years," she said.

Jacqueline went on to write two sequels. *Maizon at Blue Hill* deals with racism as it follows Maizon to the boarding school, where she is the only African American student. *Between Madison and Palmetto* catches up with Margaret and Maizon when they are finally reunited, though they question whether their friendship is as strong as it had been.

Besides the *Maizon* books, Jacqueline would go on to write more than two dozen novels for children, young adults, and even adults. Most of them would deal with controversial topics, and many of them would win prestigious awards.

The Coretta Scott King Honor book *I Hadn't Meant to Tell You This*, about a wealthy black girl's friendship with a poor white girl, deals with issues of friendship, race, and abuse.

Chapter 4
ACCOLADES ABOUND

Jacqueline's career took off like a shot. She was publishing books at an amazing pace. She tends to be a fast writer once she has her first inspiration of the characters. However, she does admit that the story in some books may not come as easily as those in others. One book was finished in just a few weeks, which was followed by one that took four years to complete. She also has a knack for writing several books simultaneously. When she gets a little tired of one for some reason (either she isn't feeling inspired, something isn't working quite right, or a new idea calls out to her), she can temporarily drop one novel and turn her attention to another. Usually, Jacqueline has three or four books in progress at any one time.

After several novels were hailed with good reviews, Jacqueline suddenly had two books in a row receive major awards. Both *I Hadn't Meant to Tell You This* (published in 1994) and *From the Notebooks of Melanin Sun* (published in 1995) were named as Coretta Scott King Honor books. The award recognizes the best African American authors who show "an appreciation of African American culture and universal human values." One author is chosen as the overall winner, and several are picked to receive a secondary "honor" qualification. To be included anywhere on the list is a high achievement.

I Hadn't Meant to Tell You This is about the friendship between two girls, one a wealthy, privileged African American, the other poor and white. They become especially close, because both have absent mothers. Like many of Jacqueline's novels, it explores issues of race, but it also treads in controversial territory with the terrible secret of abuse.

From the Notebooks of Melanin Sun also deals with race, and adds sexuality to the mix. Thirteen-year-old African American Melanin Sun is very close to his mom—she's the only family he has. When she tells him that she is gay—and when he learns that her girlfriend is white—he has to deal with his feelings of anger and confusion until he learns some truths about acceptance and love.

Soon, nearly every one of her books was wining literary prizes. One of her most famous books is the 2000 novel *Miracle's Boys*. In the following year, this realistic, moving book won the prestigious Coretta Scott King award.

The narrator of *Miracle's Boys* is twelve-year-old Lafayette, the youngest of three brothers living in the Washington Heights neighborhood of Brooklyn. When he was a little boy, his father died saving a woman and her dog after they plunged through the ice over a lake in Central Park. More recently, Lafayette's mother died of complications from diabetes. At the time of the novel, he's being raised by his oldest brother Ty'ree, who gave up a scholarship

CORETTA SCOTT KING— THE FIRST LADY OF THE CIVIL RIGHTS MOVEMENT

Coretta Scott King, the widow of slain civil rights leader Martin Luther King, Jr., was an activist and author who is the namesake of the Coretta Scott King Award for outstanding African American authors and illustrators who create books for young people.

Mrs. King worked side by side with her husband during the Civil Rights Movement. After her husband was assassinated in 1968, she took on a leading role in the movement for racial equality. In fact, she fought for universal equality, also speaking up for the women's movement and for LGBT rights. No group, she thought, should be persecuted or kept down.

In a 1998 speech, Mrs. King called upon civil rights leaders to expand their mission, and battle homophobia. She said, "Homophobia is like racism and anti-Semitism and other forms of bigotry in that it seeks to dehumanize a large group of people, to deny their humanity, their dignity, their personhood." If one minority group is allowed to be victimized, she said, then any minority group can be victimized. Equality is for everyone.

to the Massachusetts Institute of Technology to raise his younger siblings. Complicating matters is the middle brother, fifteen-year-old Charlie, who has just arrived home from a two-year stint in juvenile detention after committing armed robbery. Lafayette calls him "Newcharlie" because although he left as a gentle boy who wept for stray dogs, he has returned home empty and mean, a different person.

It is a gritty book with a deep heart, dealing with issues of loss, belonging, poverty, race, and gang violence. Despite all that, the book ends happily and hopefully. This is something that can be said of most of Jacqueline's books. No matter how bleak the situation, there is always at least a ray of hope by the end of the novel.

Miracle's Boys was so popular that it was made into a six-part television miniseries in 2005. Several people were responsible for directing the series, including noted director Spike Lee and actor/director LeVar Burton. Oddly enough, around the same time LeVar Burton was directing Jacqueline's young adult novel, he was filming a segment for his other job as host of the PBS show *Reading Rainbow*, featuring one of Jacqueline's picture books.

Jacqueline was very involved with the production process of the show—maybe too involved, she thinks. Looking back on the experience, she said, "I spent a lot of time on the set of *Miracle's Boys* when I should have been writing, and I don't want to do it again." Next time one of her projects becomes a series or film, she said, she'll probably enjoy the process from afar and keep her focus on her own work.

The list of awards bestowed on Jacqueline's work keeps growing. Three of Jacqueline's novels have been Newbery Honor books. (As with the Coretta Scott King Honor books, one primary Newbery medalist is selected, while several other books win runner-up awards.) Jacqueline is also a prolific picture book author, and one of her picture books, *Show Way*, garnered a Newbery Honor in 2006. This book depicts the journey from slavery to freedom, from segregation to equality, through several generations of a single family who all pass on the tradition of the "show way" quilt. These quilts used secret patterns to help show slaves the way to freedom. Jacqueline herself is even a character in the book, pictured at the end with her daughter, Toshi Georgiana.

Jacqueline's next Newbery Honor was awarded for *Feathers*. The title was inspired by an Emily Dickinson poem that begins,

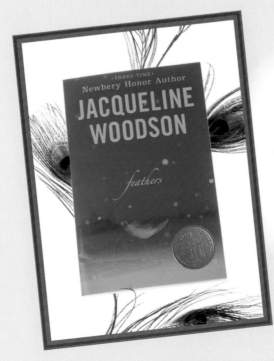

The Newbery Honor-winning *Feathers*, set in the Vietnam War era, is about the fragility and strength of hope.

THE UNDERGROUND RAILROAD AND "SHOW WAY" QUILTS

In the nineteenth century, slaves hoping to escape from the south to the northern free states and Canada used what was called the Underground Railroad, a secret network of paths and safe houses leading to freedom. This "railroad" guided some 100,000 slaves to freedom. "Conductors," who included current slaves, former slaves who returned to the south to help others, and abolitionists, guided escapees along secret routes to "stations" or "depots" where they could rest and hide along their journey. The network sometimes used codes to keep their purpose hidden. One of these codes, according to Jacqueline Woodson and others, used the designs in quilts to point out directions and landmarks. These quilts are the basis for her book, *Show Way*.

Some historians argue that there isn't enough evidence to show that quilts were used for codes. Jacqueline takes issue with these skeptics. Her grandmother had spoken about her grandmother, who passed down the story of the family's "show way" quilts. When someone said that there is no written documentation about the quilts, Jacqueline pointed out that, "The history of African Americans is oral history. We were not allowed to learn to read and write. Nobody was going to go up in the big house and say, 'Master, can you write down this story about how we're escaping using these quilts and the Underground Railroad?'"

After writing *Show Way*, Jacqueline wants to write more nonfiction as a way to record some of these historical details of the African American experience that have been passed down only in oral tradition and might otherwise be lost.

The tumbling block pattern was used in the "Show Way" quilts created for those using the Underground Railroad.

"Hope is the thing with feathers / That perches in the soul." The story takes place in the 1970s, amid protests against the Vietnam War, and is told by twelve-year-old Frannie. The story begins when a white boy enrolls in her all-black class. Jacqueline said, "*Feathers* is a book I wrote because I wanted to write about the many ways people find hope in the world."

Her most recent Newbery Honor (so far) was for the 2008 novel *After Tupac and D Foster*. An inspiring girl named D Foster changes the lives of two friends in their Queens, New York, neighborhood. She introduces them to the world beyond their own block, including the music of hip-hop artist Tupac Shakur. When Tupac is killed in a drive-by shooting, and D Foster's real mother suddenly arrives and takes her away, they find out how quickly life can change. Jacqueline said, "I thought Tupac was an amazing activist, and I wanted to create a story around his story."

Although she was barely in her fifties at the time, her body of work was so impressive that she was presented with the Margaret A. Edwards Award for Lifetime Achievement in 2006. The award, granted by the Young Adult Library Services Association and sponsored by the School Library Journal, is given to an author whose work demonstrates enduring popularity, and helps adolescents become aware of their important place in the world.

Despite all of her kudos, Jacqueline isn't used to awards yet, saying, "Every single time I win an award, I'm completely shocked. I write because I love writing, and when someone else likes it, it always catches me a little off-guard."

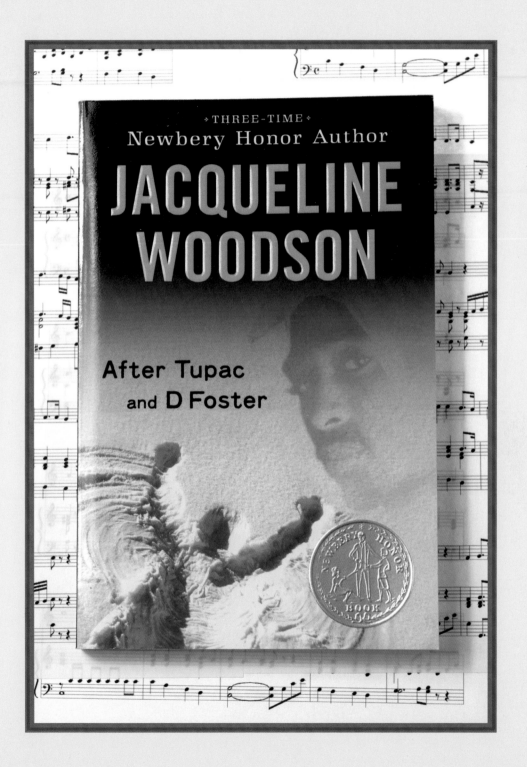

Jacqueline visited kids from the
Detroit Public School System after they
voted her their favorite author.

Chapter 5
THE OUTSIDER

As a writer (and to a certain extent, as a person) Jacqueline adopts the point of view of an outsider. Even though she was a popular child—she had a close clique of girlfriends, was a cheerleader, and dated a basketball player—she always felt she was somehow apart from all of that, being a spectator on the life she lived, looking in from the outside. So many things seemed to separate her from the rest of the world.

Race was one of the things that sometimes made her feel like an outsider. She has said, "Being African American, there are so many parts of my identity that cause me to have to step outside of any kind of mainstream." She has described walking through certain cities, where she might not see a single other person of color. Many people, she said, have a constant mirror held in front of them—they go through their lives seeing almost nothing but people who look like them. For many minorities, this is not the case. She calls being a minority a kind of invisibility.

Jacqueline believes that it is important for children to have books available that are about people who look like them but also

THE CIVIL RIGHTS MOVEMENT—
EQUALITY FOR ALL

The Civil Rights Movement in the United States took off in the 1960s, the decade in which Jacqueline was born. She grew up observing both the peaceful resistance of marches and sit-ins, and the sometimes-violent civil unrest as people fought for equal rights. One of the best-known actions, and one of the largest rallies for human rights in the history of the U.S., occurred in the year Jacqueline was born: the Great March on Washington, which gathered up to 300,000 protesters and ended with Martin Luther King, Jr.'s iconic "I Have a Dream" speech.

Following the March on Washington, the U.S. passed the Civil Rights Act of 1964, which outlawed discrimination on the basis of race, ethnicity, or gender. The following year saw the passage of the Voting Rights Act of 1965, which prohibited any discrimination in voting.

Other groups fought for equal rights in the time when Jacqueline was growing up. She witnessed firsthand the feminist movement press for such things as economic equality, educational equality, and reproductive freedom. In 1969, the Stonewall Riots in Greenwich Village, New York, brought LGBT issues to national attention. Each event increased awareness for groups struggling for equality. Today, in the United States, most people's rights are protected by law.

about people who don't. She tells a story of visiting an all-white school in Kansas. When she asked the teacher what books about African Americans she had in the classroom, the teacher replied that they didn't have any because there weren't any African American kids in class. This upset Jacqueline.

"I thought, *Are your kids always going to be here?*" she said. "When your kids leave here and they come to New York City, I don't want my child to be the first black person they encounter, because that's going to be way too foreign for them." Jacqueline thinks that children in schools that aren't diverse can still meet people of different races, socio-economic levels, and sexuality in the common ground of books.

While Jacqueline had a hard time finding books by and about people of color when she was a young girl, it isn't much easier now. A recent study found that fewer than five percent of the people traditionally published in the United States are authors of color. Most, though not all, of Jacqueline's books have main characters who are African American or biracial.

Jacqueline is also one of the few children's authors who is out as a lesbian. She has been a vocal activist for the LGBT community, and several of her books feature gay characters. Still, it makes her uncomfortable to be defined by any one thing. As she says, "It makes me nervous when an identity tries to push the others away as opposed to letting me be a writer first."

She's found her place in the world as a person and as a writer. Through her books, she hopes to help children find their own sense of belonging. Though all of her stories are vastly different, dealing with everything from teenage pregnancy to homophobia, she says they are all ways in which she is trying to work through the same story. In her twenties and thirties, she found herself moving from a place of isolation to one of belonging. "And so," she said, "I think I'm telling that story again and again in different ways and constantly figuring it out maybe just a little more deeply than the last time."

Her books are often described as "issue books" or "message books," but Jacqueline thinks her books address universal questions of identity, history, and belonging. "I don't think I have a message aside from what I believe myself," she said, "which is that we all have a right to be here, and trying to show the many ways that people can be here and be whole."

That's the idea that she is always trying to reinforce in herself, in her two children, in the community, and, of course, in her books. It's the reason why she is a writer. Writing, she says, is like her super power—one with the ability to transform her and her readers. As Jacqueline puts it, "This is what I know how to do in order to feel powerful and to make others feel powerful."

BOOKS BY JACQUELINE WOODSON

Last Summer with Maizon (1991)

The Dear One (1991)

Maizon at Blue Hill (1992)

Between Madison and Palmetto (1993)

I Hadn't Meant to Tell You This (1994)

From the Notebooks of Melanin Sun (1995)

If You Come Softly (1998)

Lena (1999)

Miracle's Boys (2000)

The Other Side (2001)

Hush (2002)

Our Gracie Aunt (2002)

Visiting Day (2002)

Locomotion (2003)

Behind You (2004)

Coming on Home Soon (2004)

Show Way (2005)

Feathers (2007)

Sweet, Sweet Memory (2007)

We Had a Picnic This Sunday Past (2007)

After Tupac and D Foster (2008)

Peace, Locomotion (2009)

Pecan Pie Baby (2010)

Beneath a Meth Moon (2012)

Each Kindness (2012)

This is the Rope: A Story from the Great Migration (2013)

GLOSSARY

civil rights movement—a social and political movement to provide equality under the law for minority groups or those suffering from discrimination. The phrase often refers to the African American Civil Rights Movement that peaked in the 1960s, but can also refer to movements to ensure rights for other minority groups, women, and the LGBT community.

Coretta Scott King Award—an annual award for outstanding African American authors and illustrators

dilettante—a person who dabbles in a subject or artistic field without truly dedicating themselves to it or gaining full knowledge

editor—a person who works to improve the quality of a piece of writing—an editor is usually the employee of a publishing company who first reads and then decides to buy an author's novel

homophobia—a range of negative feelings and actions, including discrimination and violence, toward homosexual people or behavior

LGBT—an acronym for "lesbian, gay, bisexual, and transgender"

literary agent—a person who represents writers and their books, facilitating the sale of books to publishers, movie producers, and others, in return for a commission

Newbery Medal—an award given each year for the best children's books. One book is selected to receive the medal, while between one and five are named Newbery Honor books

plagiarism—using another writer's work as if it were one's own; stealing or copying another's words or ideas without proper attribution

sharecropper—a tenant who farms land that someone else owns and gives the owner a share of the harvested crops in return

CHRONOLOGY

February 12, 1963: Jacqueline Woodson is born in Columbus, Ohio.

August 1963: During the Great March on Washington, Martin Luther King, Jr. gives his "I Have a Dream" speech.

1965: Jacqueline appears in ads for Alaga Syrup that run in *Ebony* magazine.

1965: The three Selma to Montgomery marches take place, in support of voting rights.

1968: Martin Luther King, Jr. is assassinated.

1969: The Stonewall Riots in New York City bring national attention to LGBT rights.

1973: Jacqueline first receives recognition for her writing, for a poem about Martin Luther King, Jr.

1981–1984: Jacqueline attends Adelphi University.

1991: *Last Summer with Maizon* is published.

1995: *I Hadn't Meant to Tell You This* receives a Coretta Scott King Honor.

1996: *From the Notebooks of Melanin Sun* receives a Coretta Scott King Honor.

1995–6: Jacqueline is a writer-in-residence with the National Book Foundation.

2001: *Miracle's Boys* wins the Coretta Scott King Award.

2004: *Locomotion* receives a Coretta Scott King Honor.

2005: *Miracle's Boys* is made into a six-part television miniseries.

2006: *Show Way* wins a Newbery Honor.

2006: Jacqueline wins the Margaret Edwards Award for lifetime achievement in children's writing.

2008: *Feathers* wins a Newbery Honor.

2009: *After Tupac and D Foster* wins a Newbery Honor.

2013: The Defense of Marriage Act is ruled unconstitutional, paving the way for many U.S. states to make same-sex marriage legal.

FURTHER INFORMATION

Books

Fletcher, Ralph. *A Writer's Notebook: Unlocking the Writer Within You.* New York, NY: HarperCollins, 2003.

Levine, Gail Carson. *Writing Magic: Creating Stories that Fly.* New York, NY: HarperCollins, 2006.

Messner, Kate. *Real Revision: Authors' Strategies to Share with Student Writers.* Portland, ME: Stenhouse Publishers, 2011.

Website

Jacqueline Woodson's home page

www.jacquelinewoodson.com/

Jacqueline Woodson's website, updated frequently by the author herself, has a ton of great resources for students and those who read for fun. Here you can find information on her life, her work, her awards, upcoming projects, and more. You can also find links to her Facebook and Twitter pages.

INDEX

ABOUT THE AUTHOR:

Laura L. Sullivan is a prolific author of books for children and young adults. Her novels include the fantasies *Under the Green Hill* and *Guardian of the Green Hill*, as well as the historical novels *Ladies in Waiting* and *Love by the Morning Star*. She is also the author of *Spotlight on Children's Authors: Gail Carson Levine* for Cavendish Square. Her favorite books by Jacqueline Woodson are *Show Way* and *Miracle's Boys*.